PART ONE

TIMES FABLES

HOW TO USE THIS BOOK

This book contains all the information you need to learn your 3, 4, 6, 7, 8 and 9 times tables. It may not be the traditional way to learn your times tables, but it's lots of fun, and really does work!

Don't try to figure out how the book works. To begin with, just concentrate on learning the stories. By the time you reach the end of Part 1, all will be revealed, and you'll realise that the stories that you have learnt are really just hidden multiplication problems.

Start by memorising the characters on the next page. Can you see that each character has been drawn in such a way as to look like the number it represents?

MEET THE CHARACTERS

The stories that follow each contain exactly two of the following characters:

- The robins (can you find a number 3 hidden in each bird?)

- A chair (which is shaped like the number 4)

- Six elves (can you see that they look like little sixes?)

- Dr Sven (she's a reindeer, but she also looks like the number 7)

- Mrs Snowman (who bears a remarkable resemblance to the number 8)

- A magic tree (it must be magic, because it's shaped like the number 9)

Mrs Snowman and Dr Sven meet 5 times a week at 6 o'clock to have dinner.

On which days do you think they meet?

Would you like to have dinner with your friends 5 times a week at 6 o'clock like Mrs Snowman and Dr Sven do?

Remember, Mrs Snowman and Dr Sven meet for dinner
5 times a week at 6 o'clock.

Mrs Snowman was just about to go out when she realised she hadn't put on her 3 buttons and 2 mittens, which were sitting on the top shelf of a very tall cupboard.

How do you think Mrs Snowman reached her 3 buttons and 2 mittens?

Why, she stood on a chair, of course. How else would Mrs Snowman get her 3 buttons and 2 mittens if she didn't have a chair to stand on?

Remember, Mrs Snowman stood on a chair to reach her

3 buttons and 2 mittens.

Did you know that Santa has six elves that help him make toys for all the good boys and girls around the world?

They work in a little workshop located in the middle of a very secret magic tree.

Every year, the elves arrive at the magic tree workshop exactly 54 days before Christmas.

Remember, Santa's six Elves arrive at the magic tree workshop exactly 54 days before Christmas.

A red-breasted robin landed on a chair, and started to sing the 12 Days of Christmas.

Do you know that song?

Perhaps you could sit on your favourite chair and sing the 12 Days of Christmas, just like the robin did!

Remember, a robin landed on a chair and started to sing the 12 Days of Christmas.

Mrs Snowman was feeling hungry, so she went to the magic tree to get some fruit.

She asked the tree for 7 apples and 2 plums and gobbled them up as quickly as you can say, "Greedy Mrs Snowman!"

Do you think you'd be able to eat 7 apples and 2 plums in one go, like Mrs Snowman? I'm not sure I could!

Remember, Mrs Snowman went to the magic tree and asked for 7 apples and 2 plums.

It was break time for Santa's six elves, so they decided to play a game of musical chairs.

The six elves were having so much fun that they kept playing musical chairs for 24 hours. That's a whole day!

I wonder what Santa said when he discovered that his six elves had spent 24 hours playing musical chairs! Do you think he was cross?

Remember, the six elves played musical chairs for 24 hours.

Dr Sven was walking past the magic tree, when something suddenly caught her eye.

She took a closer look, and realised it was 63 shiny gold coins.

What do you think Dr Sven did with the 63 coins that she found at the bottom of the magic tree? Do you think she put them back where she found them? Perhaps the 63 coins are still there!

63 coins

Remember, Dr Sven found 63 coins at the bottom of the
magic tree.

Dr Sven was just about to enter the hospital where she works when all of a sudden, a robin landed on her nose, making her sneeze 21 times.

That's a lot of sneezes, isn't it? Perhaps Dr Sven is allergic to robins.

Can you think of anything that might make you sneeze 21 times?

Remember, a robin landed on Dr Sven's nose and made her sneeze 21 times.

Mrs Snowman wasn't feeling very well.

The six elves heard she was poorly and decided to check on her.

They took her temperature and found it was a very hot 48 degrees.

Do you think the six elves were worried when they discovered Mrs Snowman had a temperature of 48 degrees? That's a very high temperature, especially for a snowman.

Remember, the six elves took Mrs Snowman's temperature and found it was 48 degrees.

All of a sudden, a group of robins flew towards the magic tree.

The robins circled the tree 27 times.

Why do you think they did that? Do you suppose they were looking for something?

I bet the robins felt dizzy after flying around the tree 27 times!

Remember, a group of robins circled around the magic tree 27 times.

Dr Sven has a very busy job, and doesn't get to sit down very often. When she does, she likes to sit in her favourite chair and dream about her holiday.

Dr Sven is very excited, as she is going to Chair-land in February. For 28 days, Dr Sven plans to do nothing but sit in a chair and relax!

It sounds boring, doesn't it? But not for Dr Sven – she can't think of anything she'd rather do than spend 28 days sitting in a comfy chair!

Remember, Dr Sven is going to Chair-land in February, where

she will spend 28 days sitting in a chair!

Mrs Snowman was getting hotter and hotter.

What happens to snow when it gets hot? That's right, it melts!
Poor Mrs Snowman!

Mrs Snowman was just beginning to melt, when all of a sudden,
a group of naughty robins flew off with her 2 arms and her
4-metre long scarf.

What do you think the robins did with Mrs Snowman's 2 arms
and her 4-metre long scarf?

Remember, a group of robins flew off with Mrs Snowman's

2 arms and her 4 metre-long scarf.

The elves went to visit Dr Sven in her hospital and took with them 42 presents for each of Dr Sven's patients.

How kind of the elves to think about Dr Sven's 42 patients.

I'm sure Dr Sven's patients felt much better after seeing six elves arrive with 42 presents for them. I know I would, wouldn't you?

Remember, the six elves went to visit Dr Sven in her hospital
and took with them 42 presents for her sick patients.

Christmas is drawing nearer, and the elves are behind schedule. There are so many presents to wrap and not enough time!

The elves decide to send a message to the robins to ask if they might be able to come and help.

The elves are very pleased when the next day, a group of 18 robins turn up to help them. Now they will be able to get all the presents wrapped in time for Christmas. Hooray!

18 robins, reporting for duty!

Remember, the elves needed help preparing for Christmas,

so they sent a message to the robins, and were delighted

when a group of 18 turned up to help.

It's 3am on the 6th January and something magical is about to happen. The magic tree workshop, which is not needed for another year, is about to transform itself into a very special chair.

Don't worry though. The workshop will return next year.

But for now, it's time for Santa to put his feet up and relax. And where better to do that than in a lovely wooden chair carved out of the tree, where he has spent the past few weeks preparing for Christmas?

Remember, the magic tree workshop transformed itself into a special chair at 3 am on the 6th of January.

Believe it or not, if you can remember all the stories from the previous pages, then you now know most of your times tables!

For example, if you want to know the answer to 6 x 4, simply think of the story that includes both the six elves (number 6) and the chair (number 4) and you will find the answer hidden in the story – in this case **24**, because the **SIX ELVES** played musical **CHAIRS** for **24** hours.

Try it for yourself...

What is 8 x 6?

To get the answer, you first need to remember which character represents the number 8, and who or what represents number 6.

Next, think of the story containing these characters...

HERE'S A HINT...

The six elves took Mrs Snowman's temperature. But what was her temperature? Do you remember?

THE CORRECT ANSWER IS 48. DID YOU GET IT RIGHT?

If you didn't get the right answer, go back and re-read the

stories. When you are confident that you know them all, try to

answer the questions on the next page.

Here's some more for you to try:

4 x 3 =   8 x 7 =   9 x 7 =   8 x 4 =

6 x 8 =   9 x 4 =   4 x 6 =   9 x 6 =

7 x 6 =   3 x 8 =   7 x 3 =   4 x 9 =

6 x 9 =   7 x 4 =   6 x 8 =

PART TWO

SQUARE NUMBERS

Square numbers are those multiplied by themselves.

To learn these we don't need robins, snowmen, trees or elves.

3 times 3? Think of the rhyme,

And you'll remember that the answer is 9.

If ever you find yourself asked by the Queen,

What 4 times 4 is, please tell her 16.

High 5!
It's 25

5 times 5 is 25.

How good it is to be alive (High-Five!)

Abracadabra! Magic tricks.

6 times 6 is 36.

7 kids in 7 lines.

Add them up, it's 49.

8 times 8 is 64.

Push your (8-year-old) sister out the door.

Learning times tables is so much fun...

Just two more to go, and then we're done.

9 times 9 is 81.

Run along and eat a bun.

The easiest of all, it must be said,

10 times 10 is one hundred.

Read the square number rhymes through a few times, and

then try to answer the questions on the next page.

How many can you remember?

$3 \times 3 =$ $4 \times 4 =$ $5 \times 5 =$ $6 \times 6 =$

$7 \times 7 =$ $8 \times 8 =$ $9 \times 9 =$ $10 \times 10 =$

CONGRATULATIONS

You have completed the book, and are officially

a times tables genius!

Note to Parents

This book was written after my own child struggled to master her times tables using traditional methods. As a mathematician, I was keen that my daughter learn to love numbers as much as I do, so came up with the idea of trying to teach her the times tables through storytelling, using visual cues to help her come up with the right answer to simple multiplication problems.

The book has been split into two parts. The first section will help your child work out how the answer to multiplications involving two different numbers, ranging from 3 to 9. (Note that the 2, 5 and 10 times tables are not included in this book). These stories employ visual cues that help children quickly recall otherwise abstract sums. Encourage your child to read through the stories a few times, and then test them on the details to see how much they remember. Ask them, for example, which story involves Mrs Snowman and Dr Sven. Ask if they can remember what Mrs Snowman and Dr Sven did together in the story. You can now explain to your child that working out the answer to 7 x 8 is as simple as identifying the number hidden in the story – in this case, 56 since Dr Sven and Mrs Snowman meet 5 times a week at 6 o'clock. It sounds complicated, but it's really not!

Once your child has mastered the tables in Part 1, encourage them to move on to Part 2. This section makes use of simple rhyme to help children learn the square numbers – that is, numbers multiplied by themselves, such as 3 x 3 or 4 x 4. You might even want to encourage your child to make up their own rhymes, which is an excellent way to help reinforce the times tables.

Above all, have fun. As I hope this book demonstrates, learning times tables needn't be a chore. Sometimes all it takes is a different approach.

Times tables included in the book are: 3x3, 3x4, 3x6, 3x7, 3x8, 3x9, 4x4, 4x6, 4x7, 4x8, 4x9, 5x5, 6x6, 6x7, 6x8, 6x9, 7x7, 7x8, 7x9, 8x8, 8x9, 9x9, 10x10.

J. Wilson
Author and mathematician
www.timesfabl.es

Printed in Great Britain
by Amazon